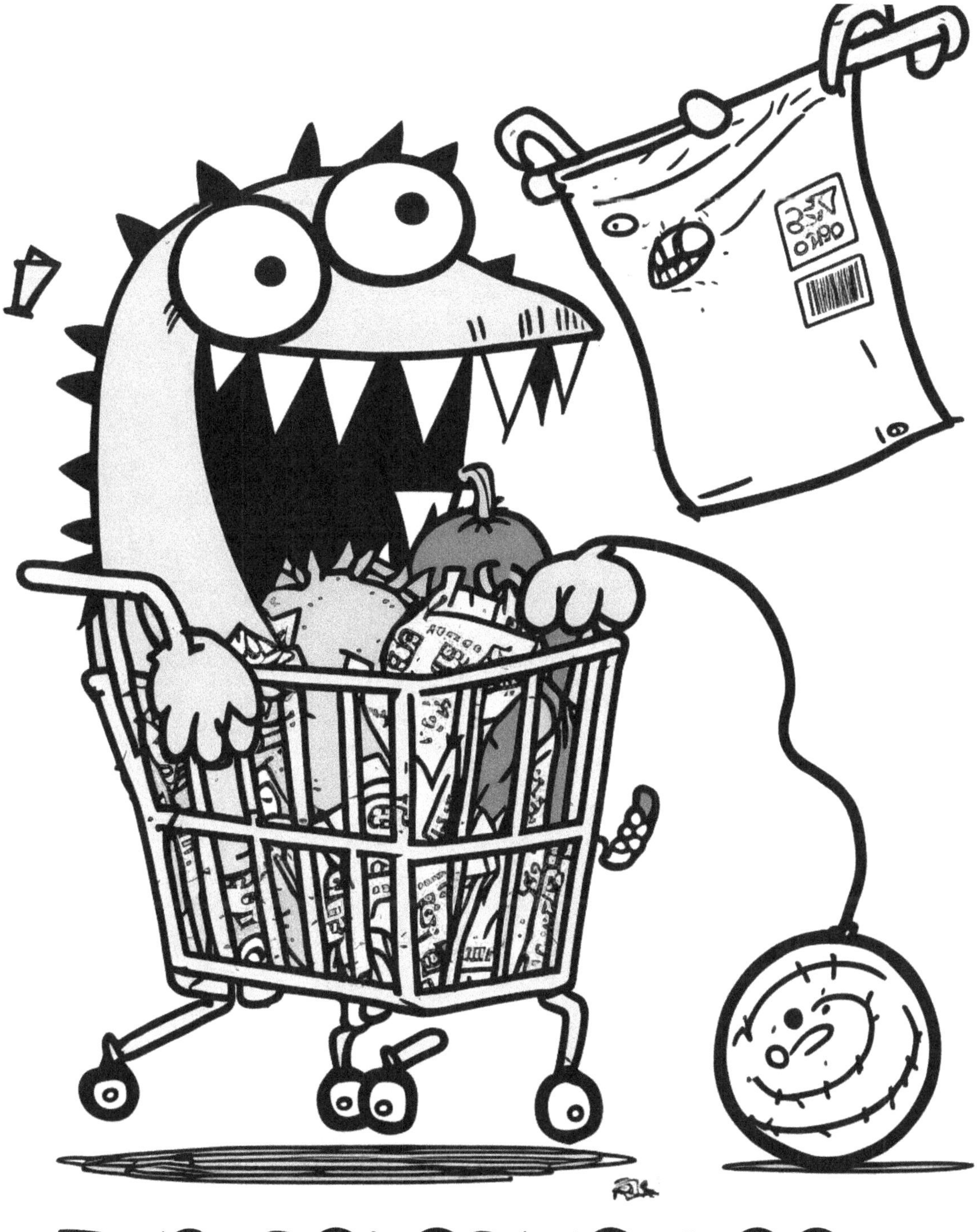

THIS COLORING BOOK BELONGS TO:

____

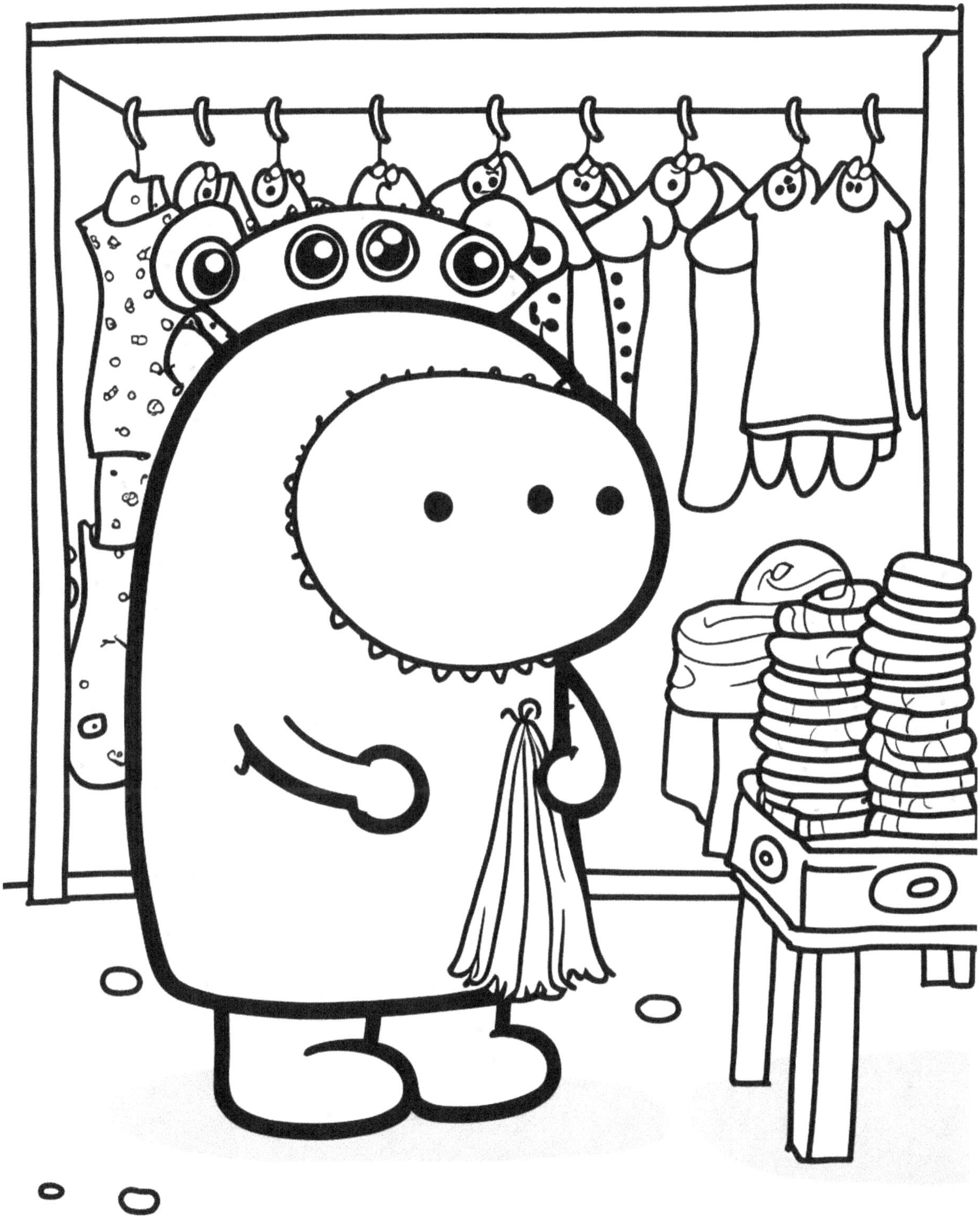

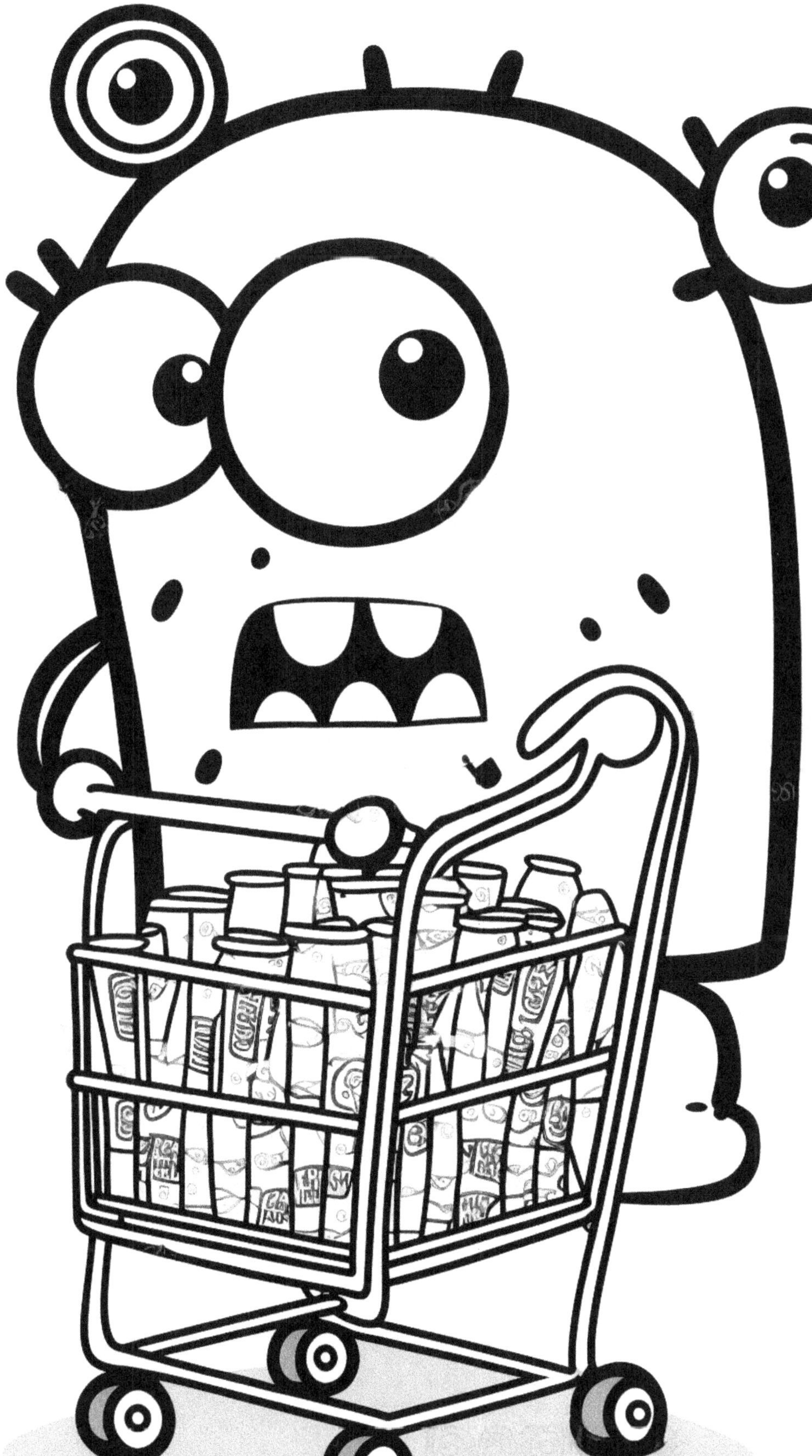

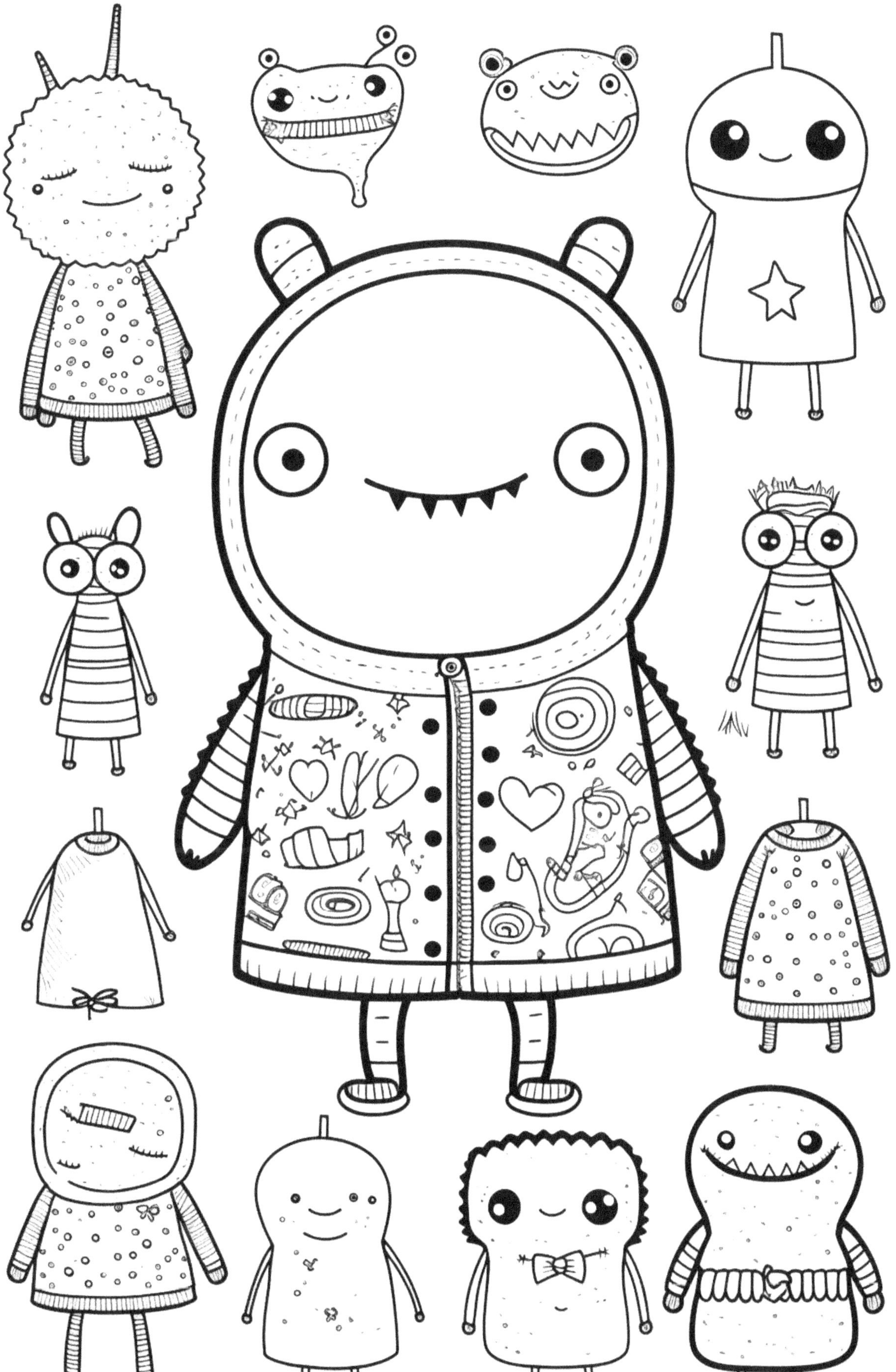

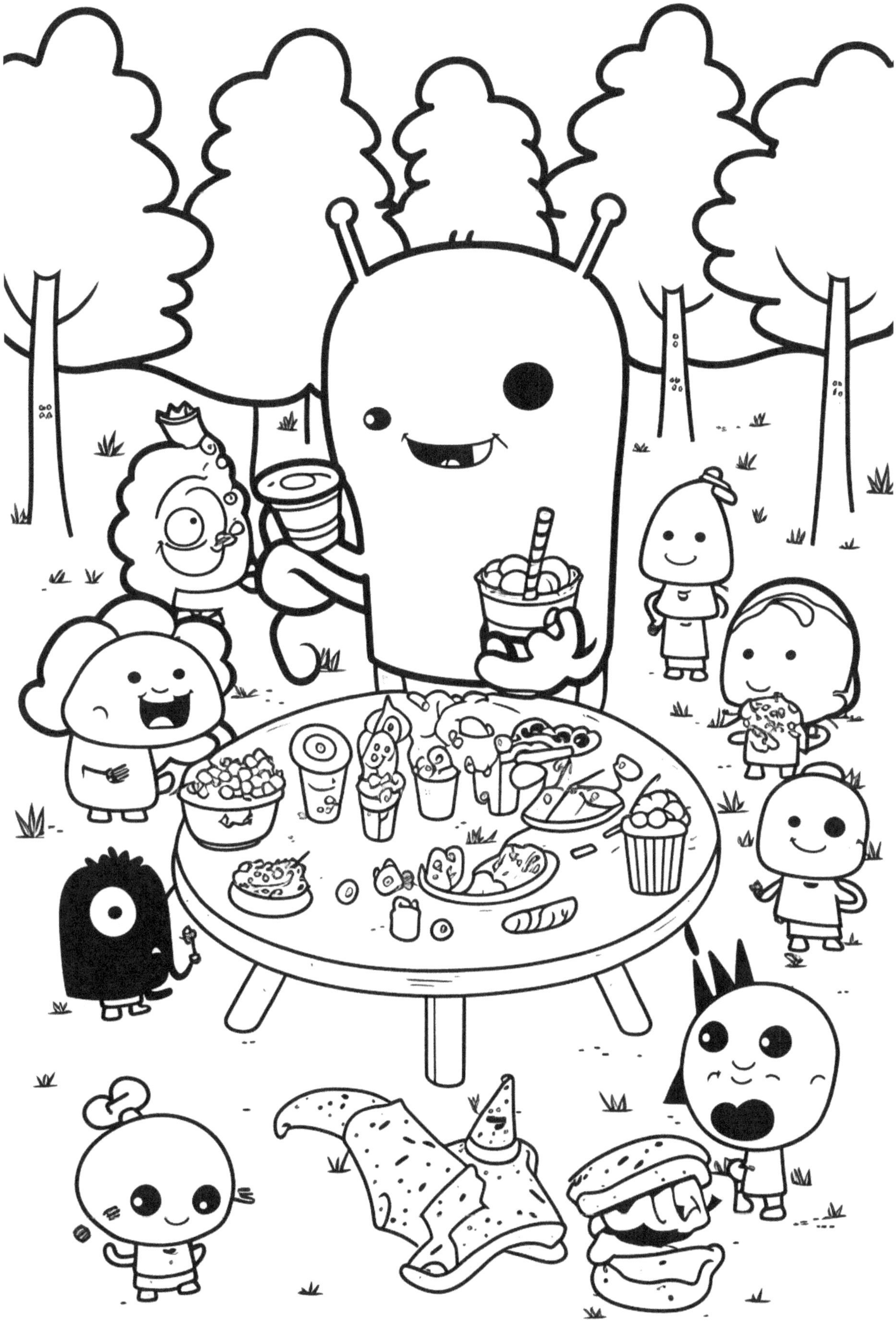

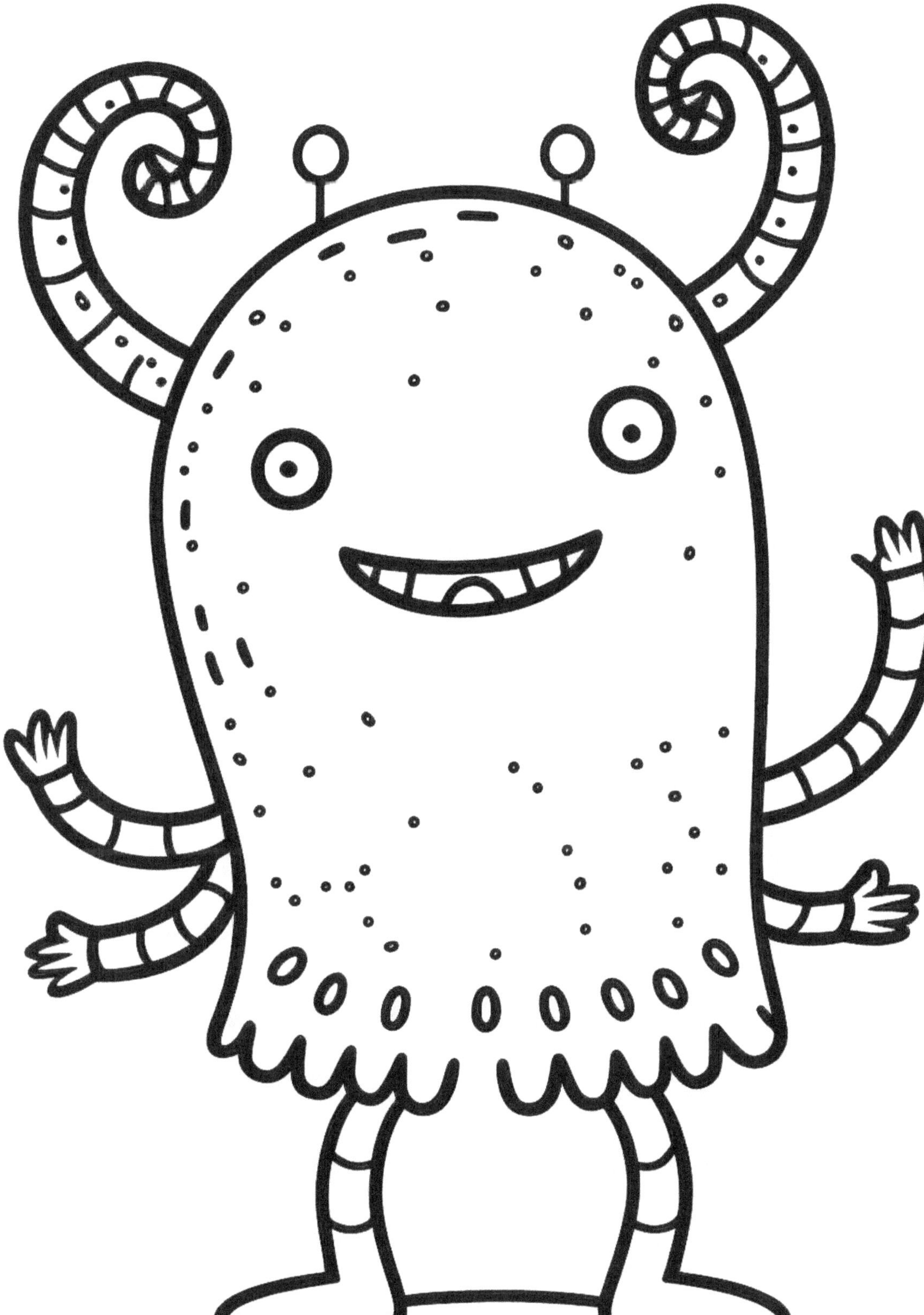

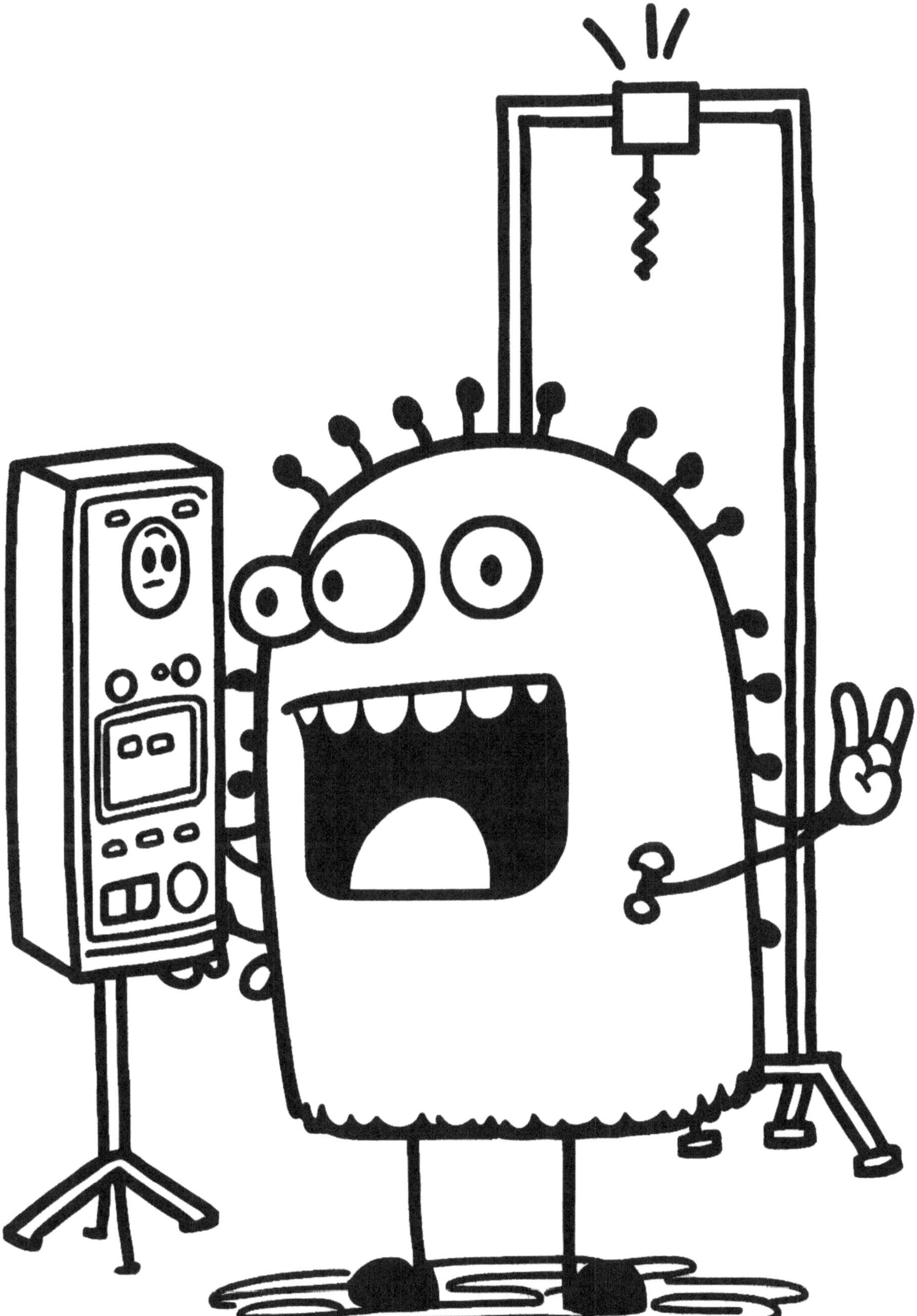

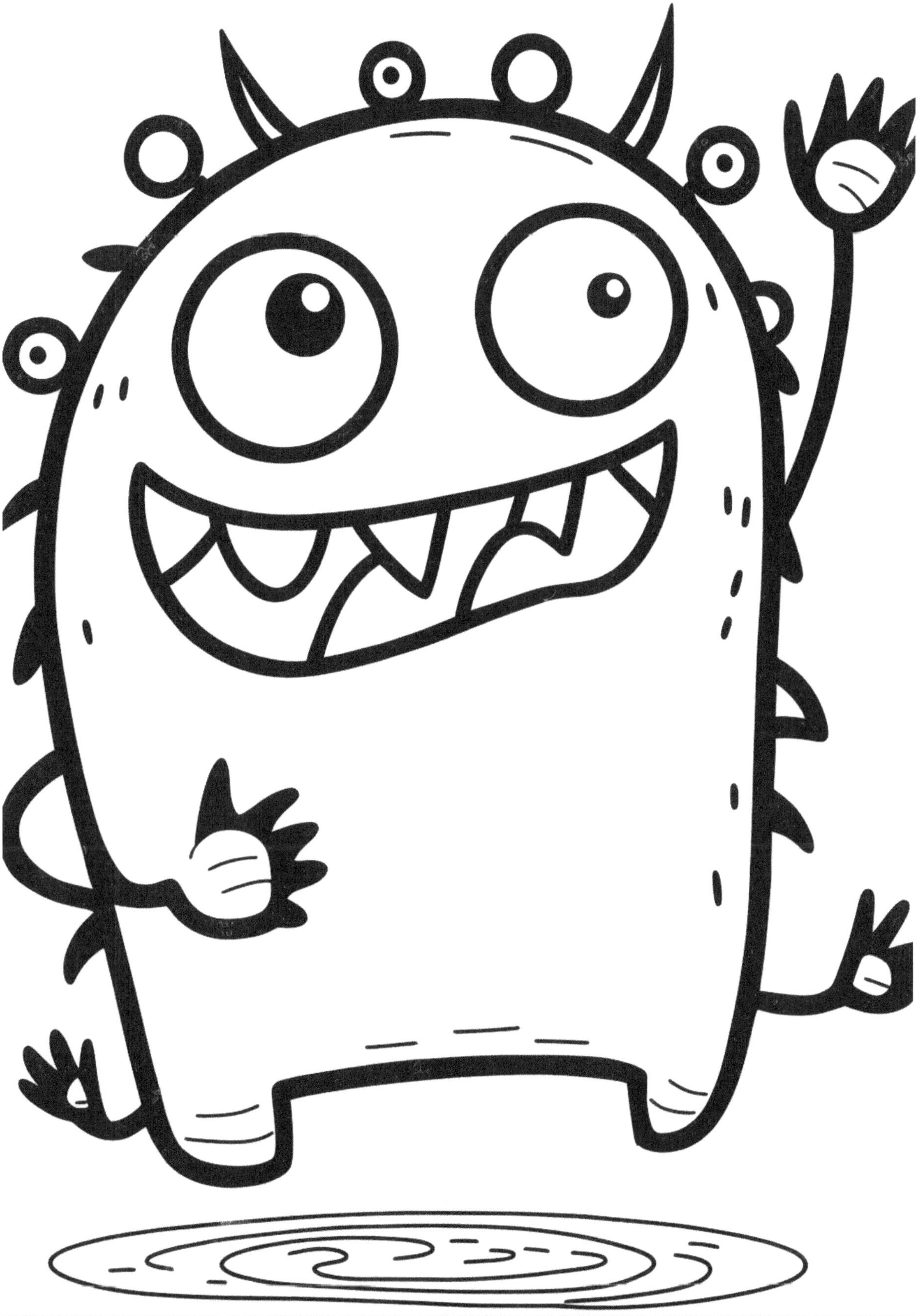

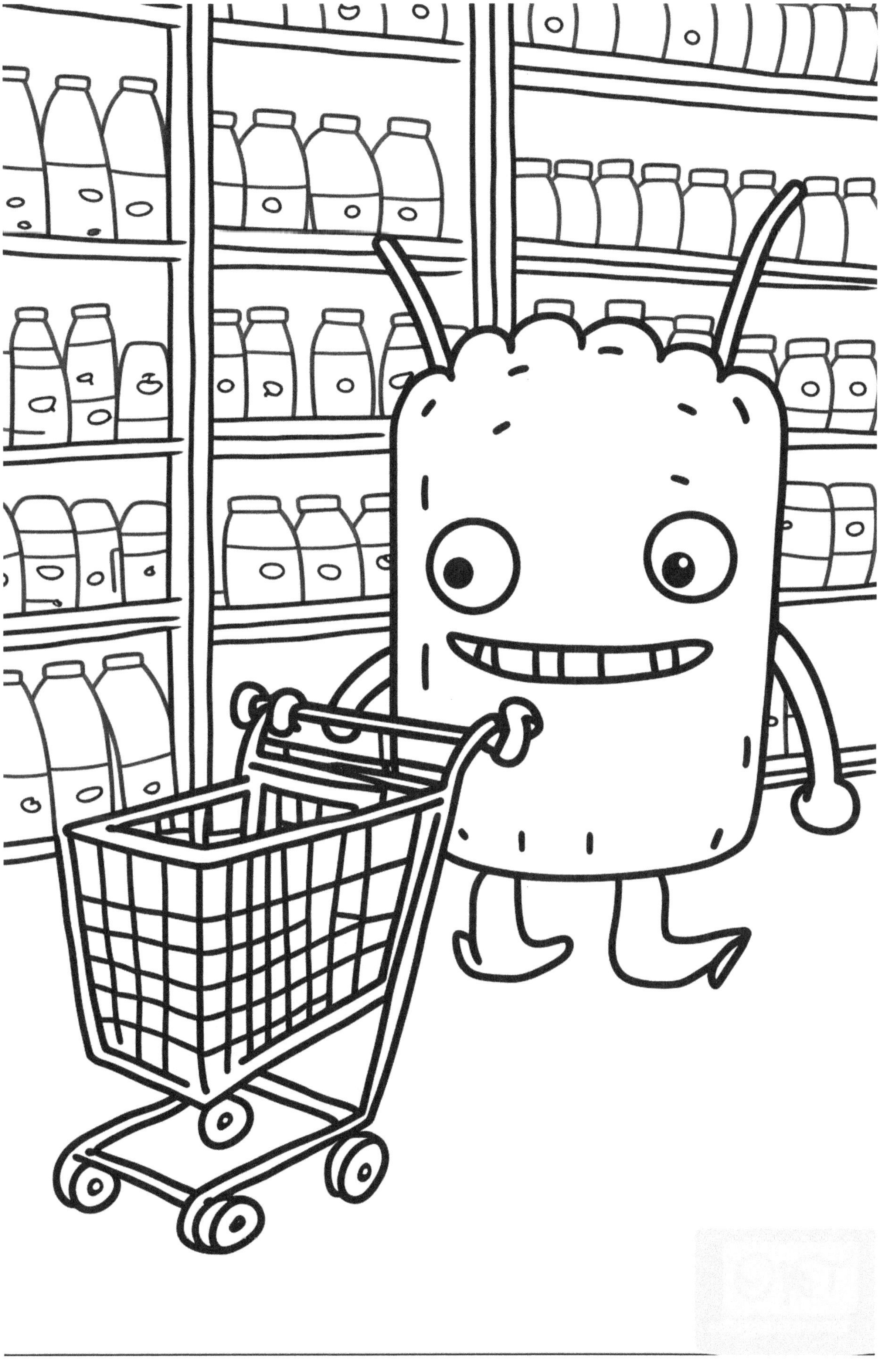

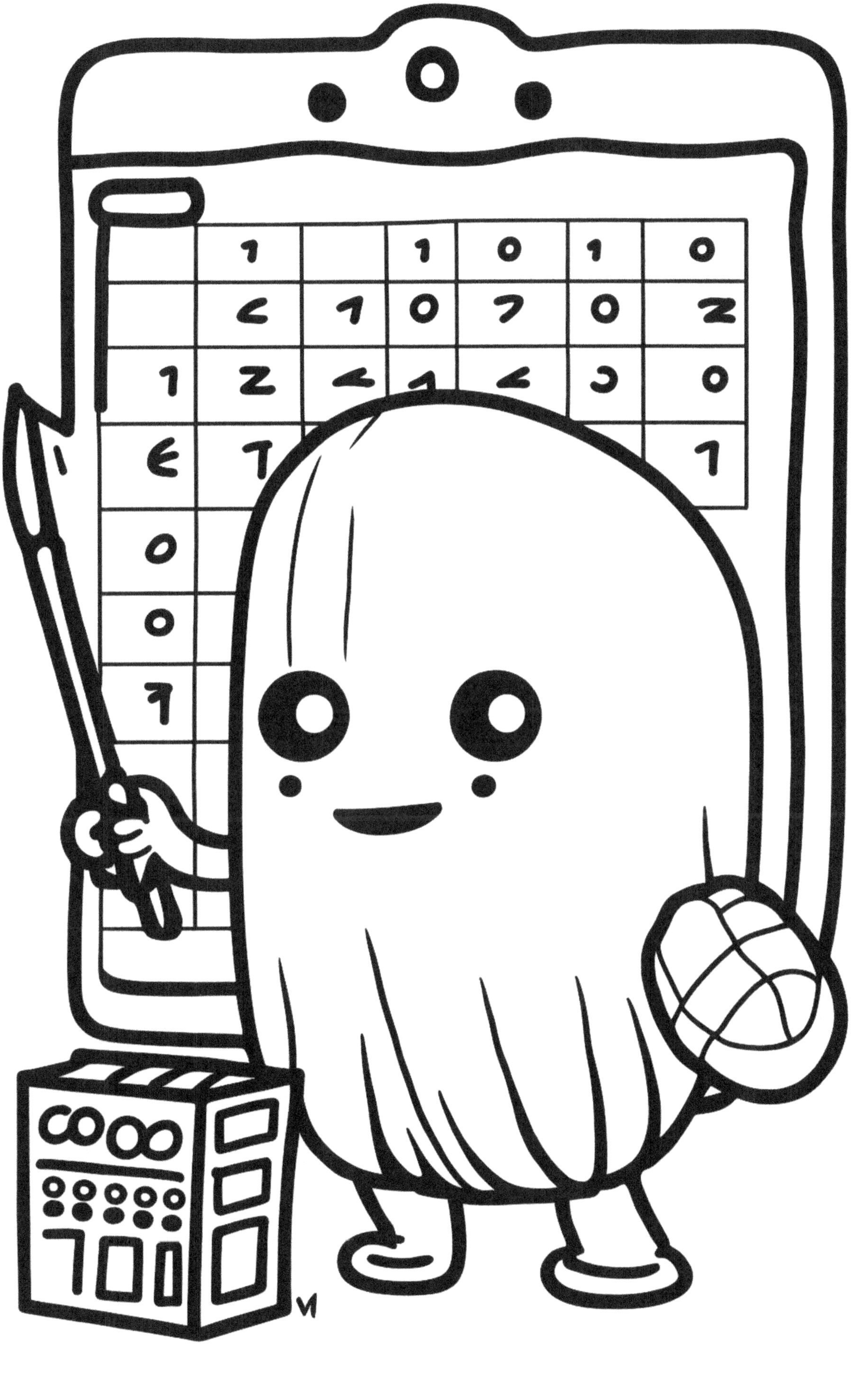

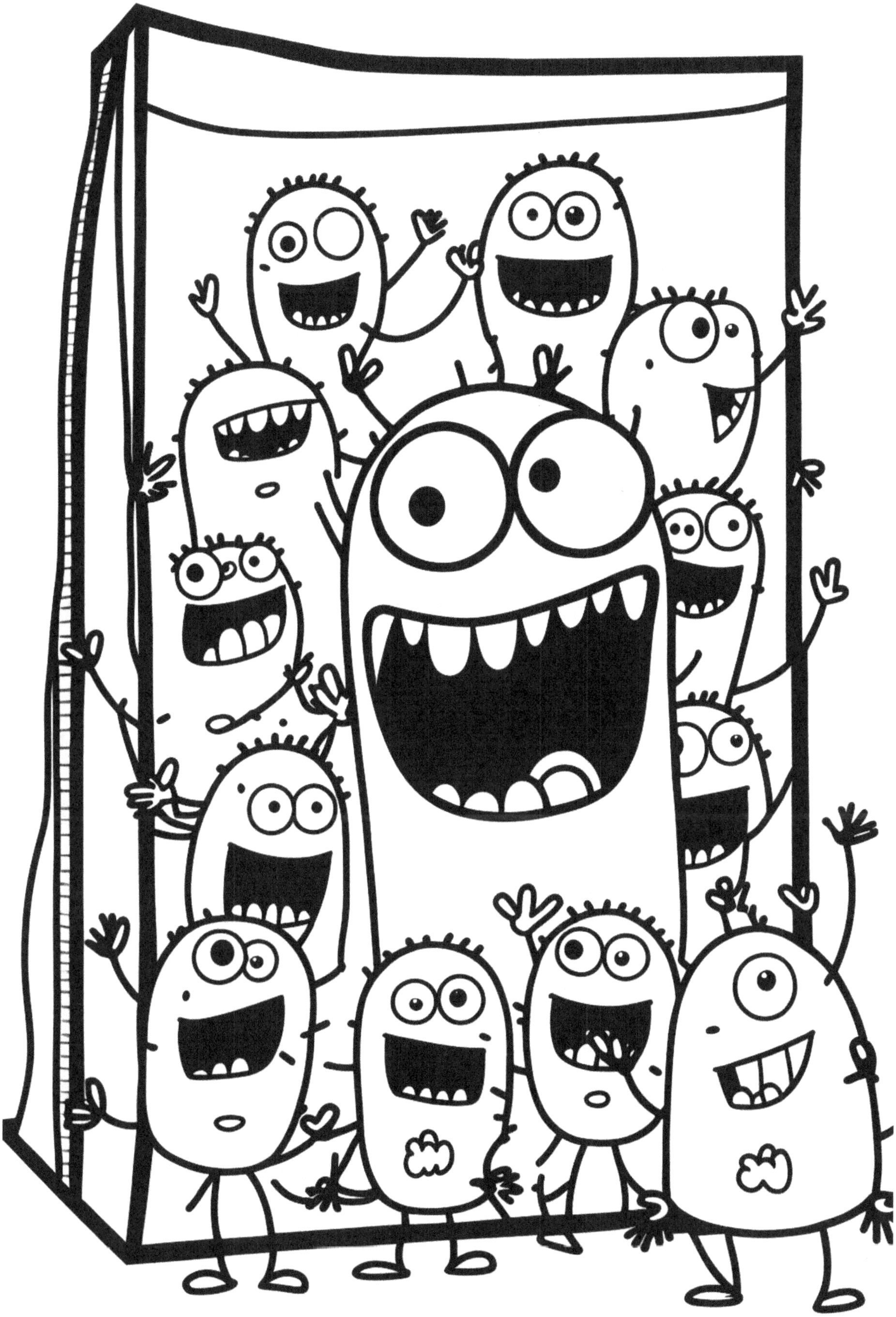

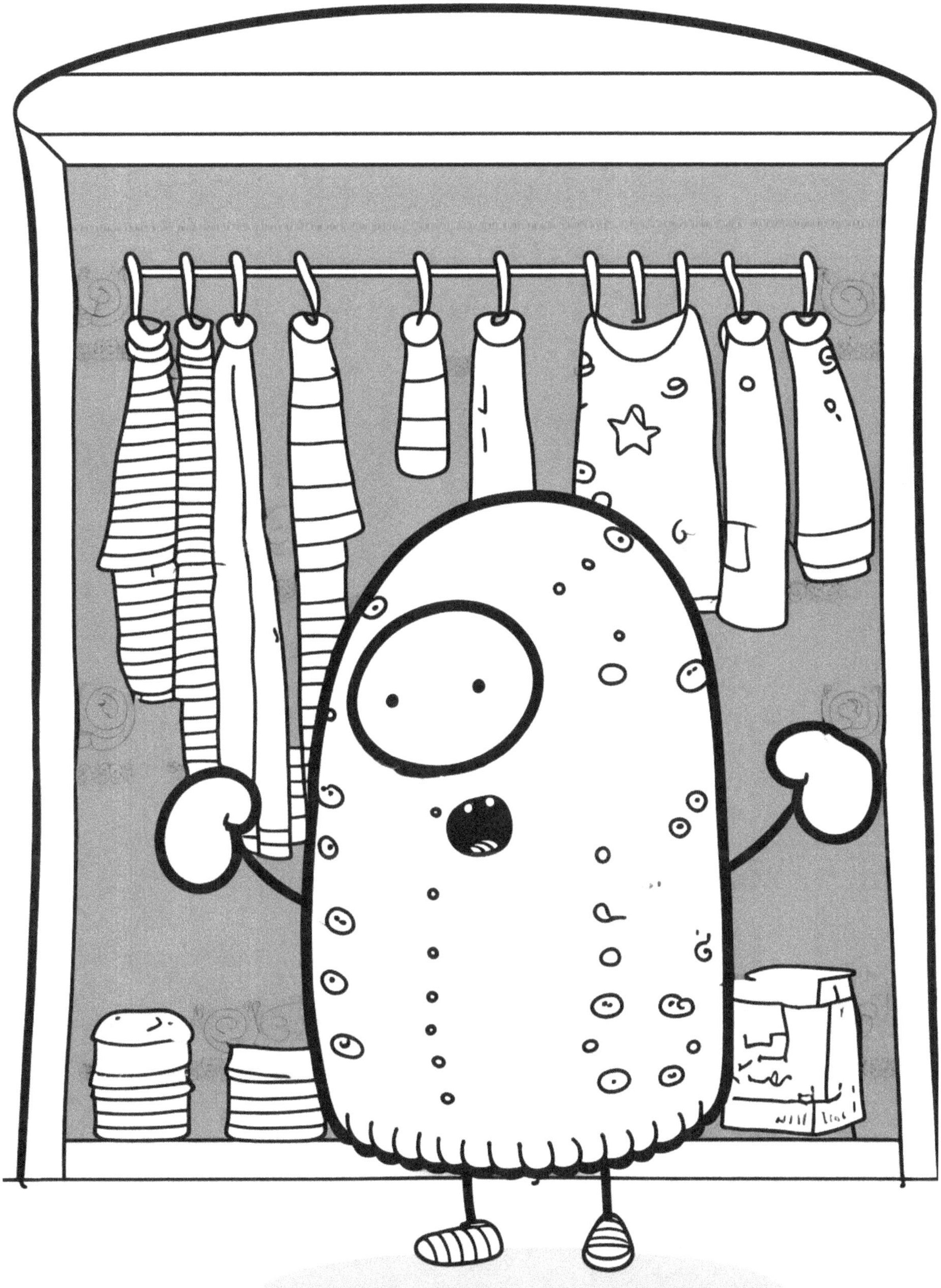

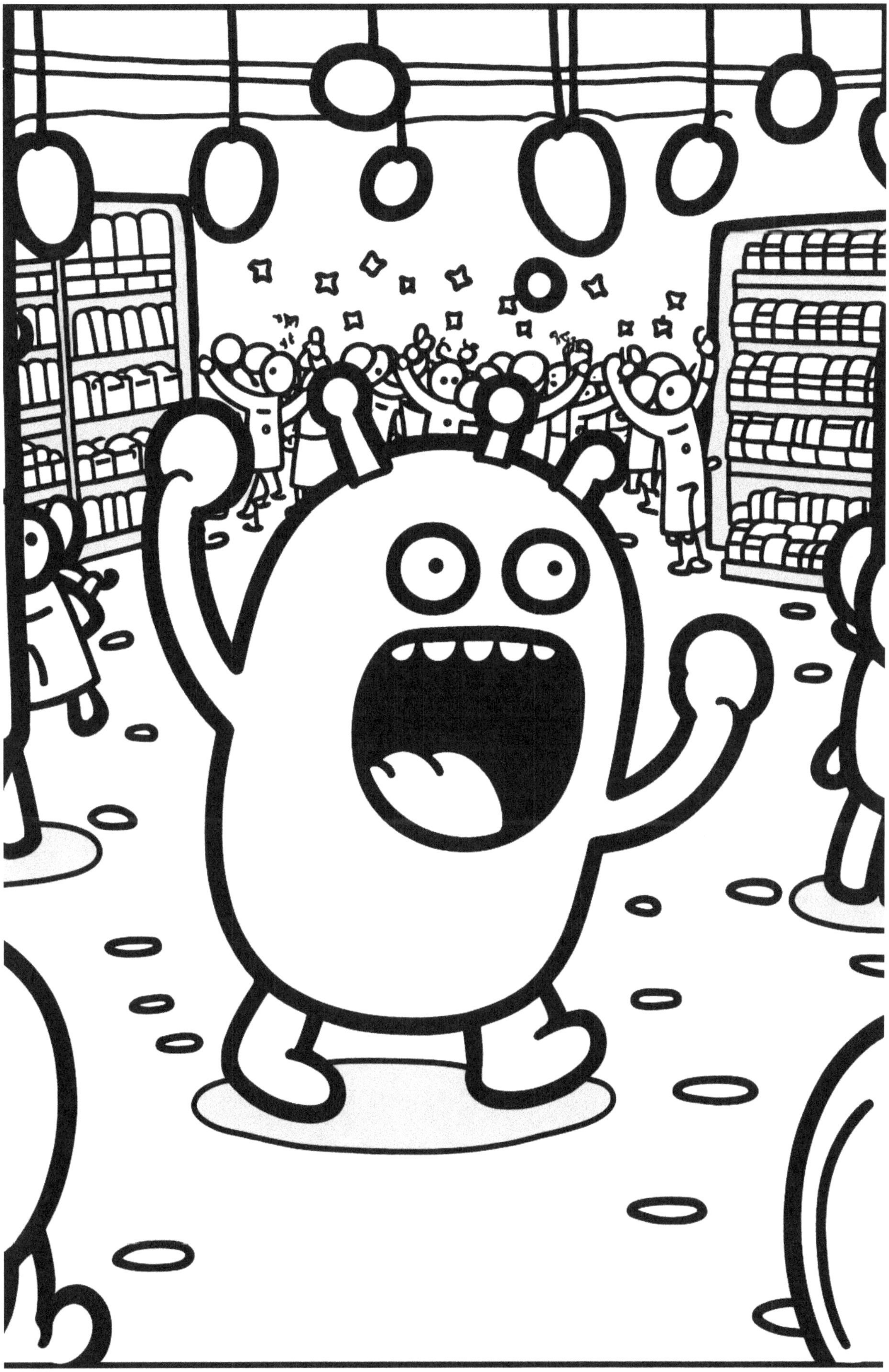

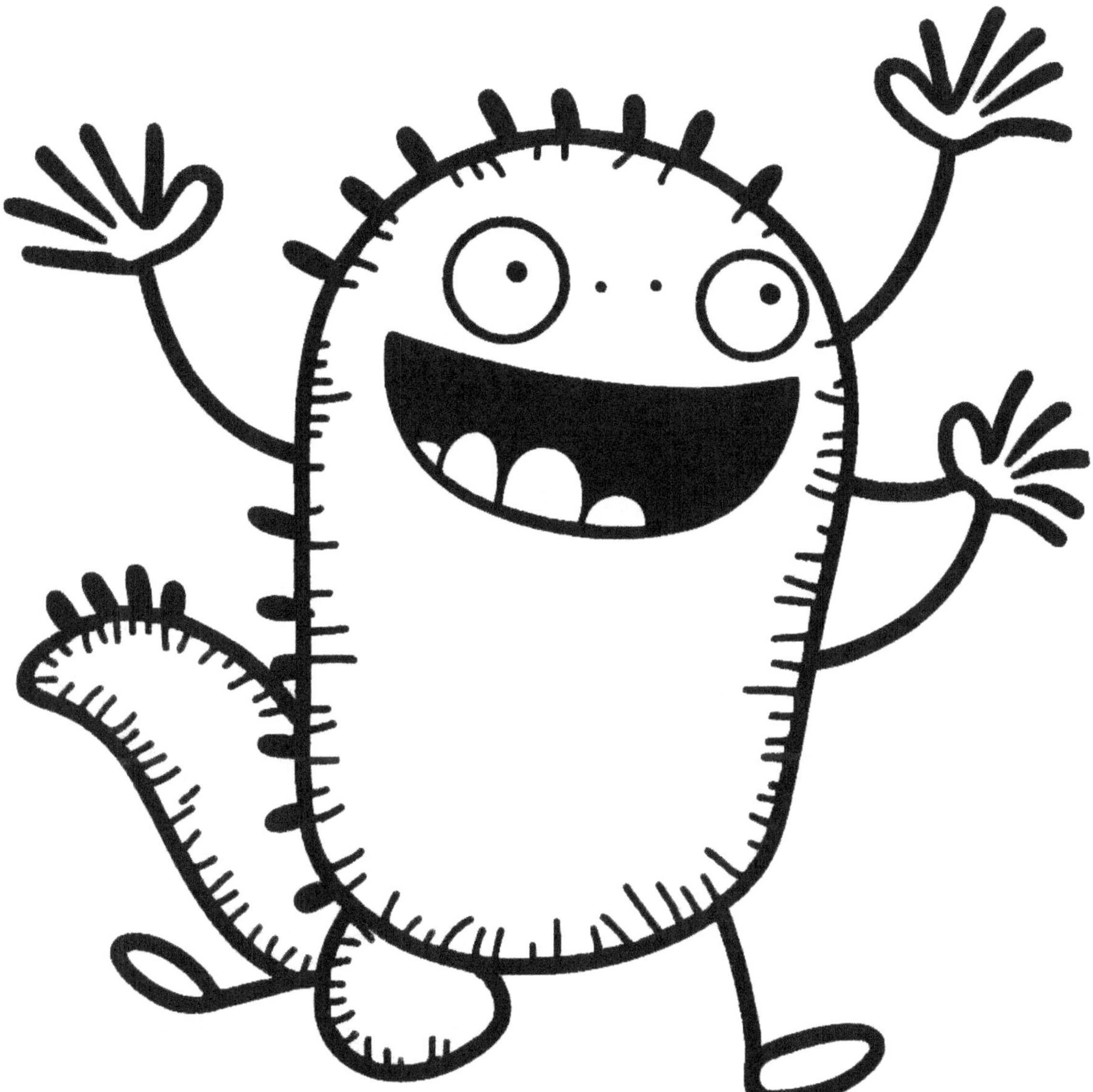

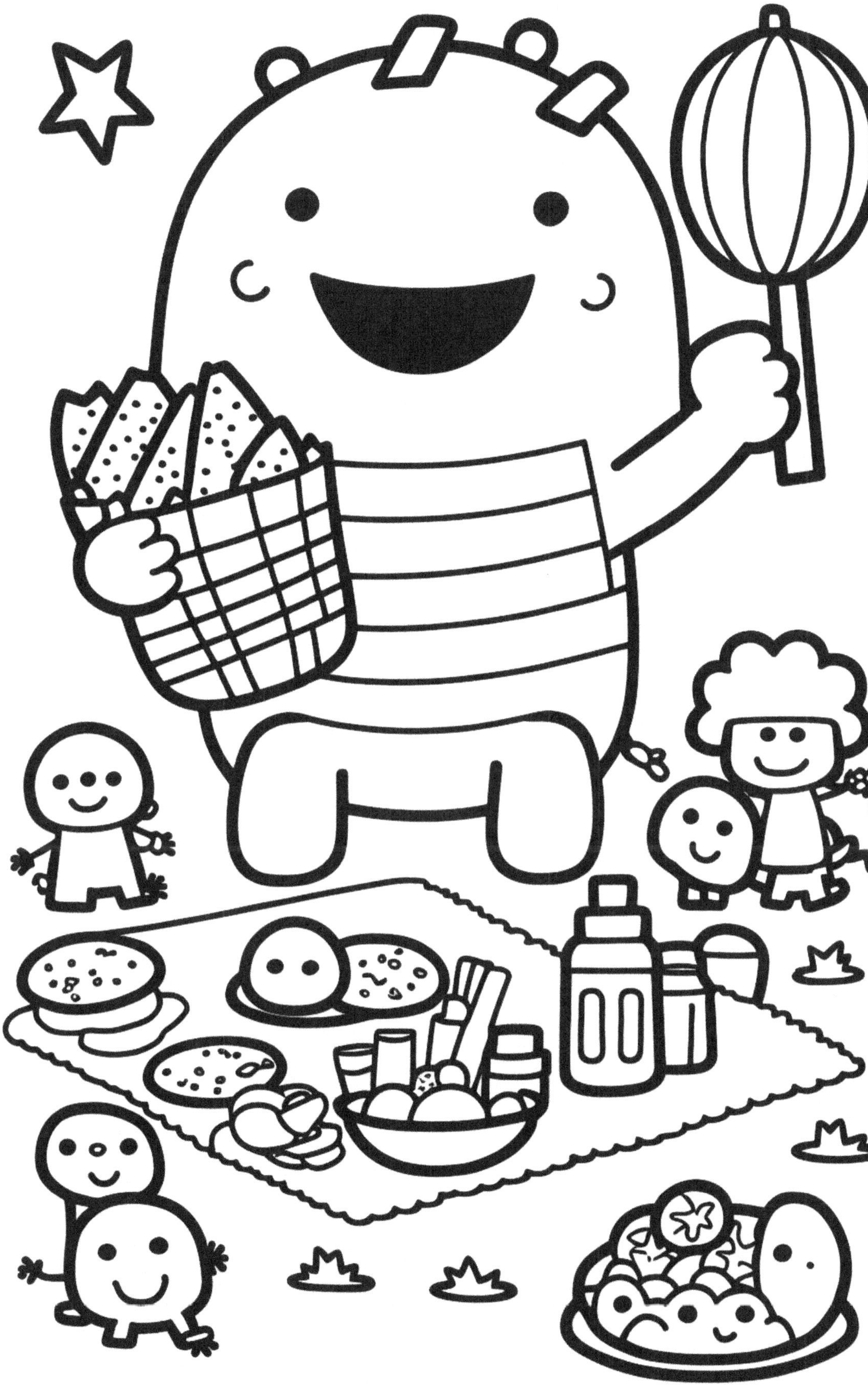

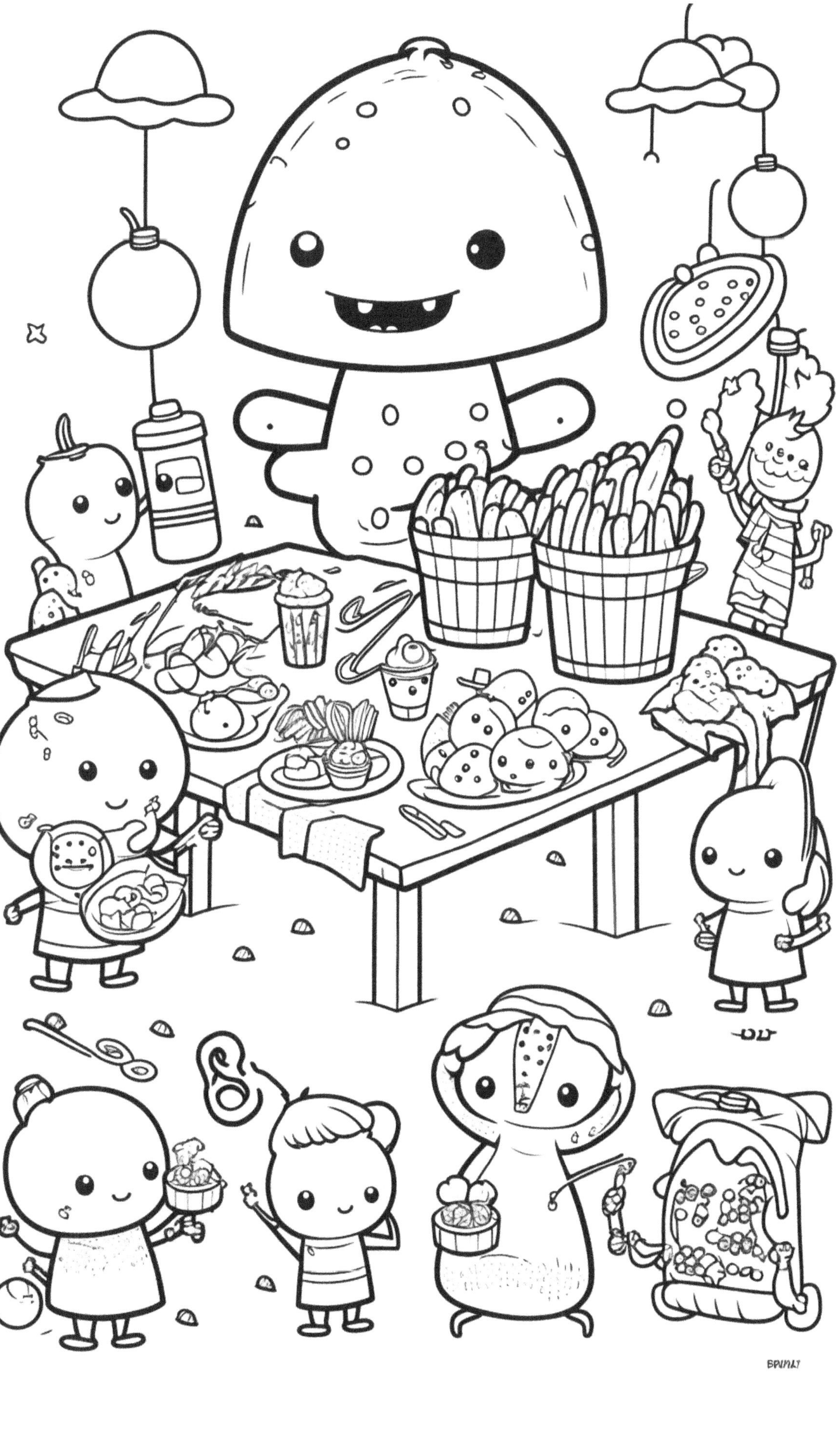

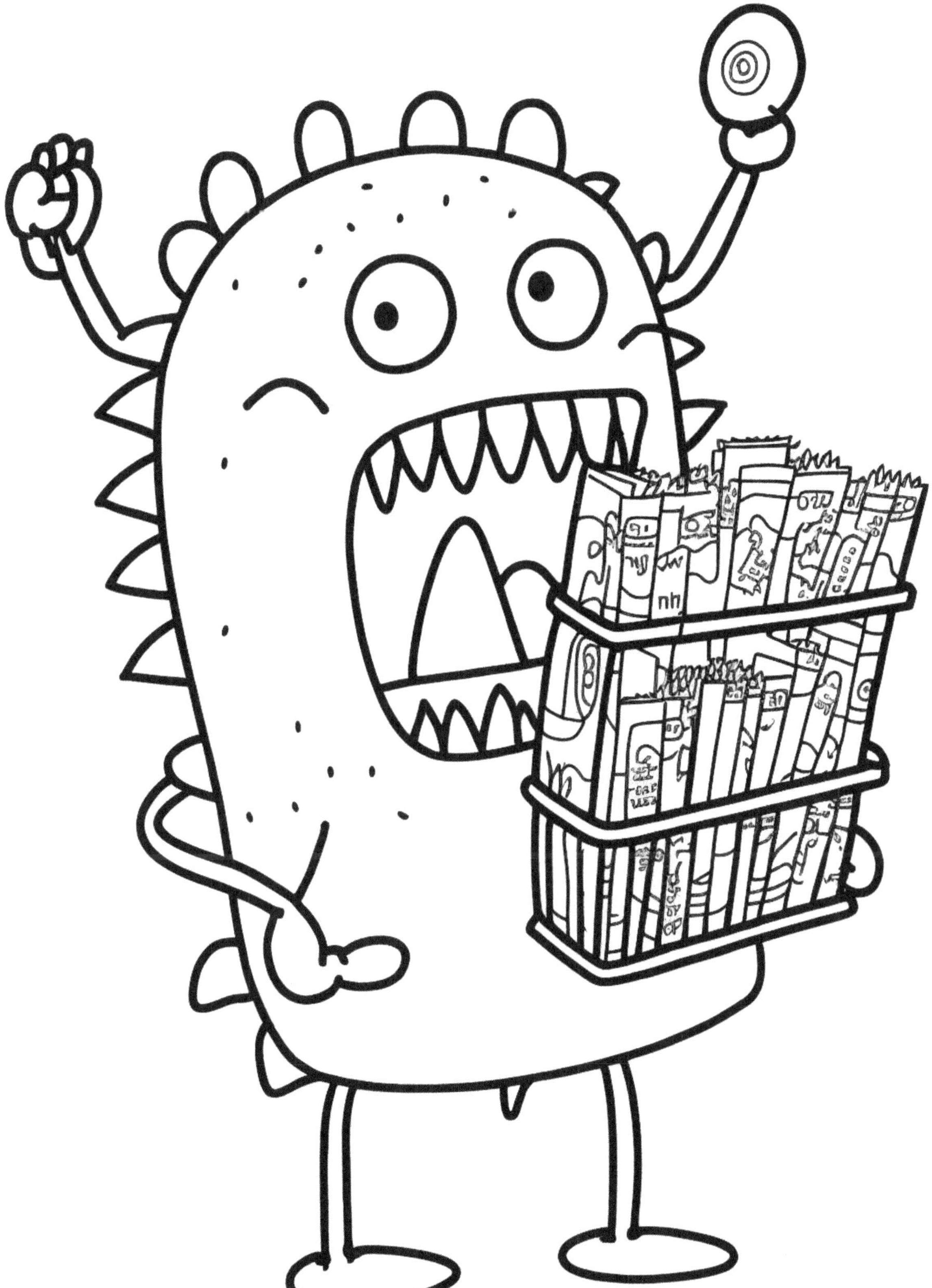

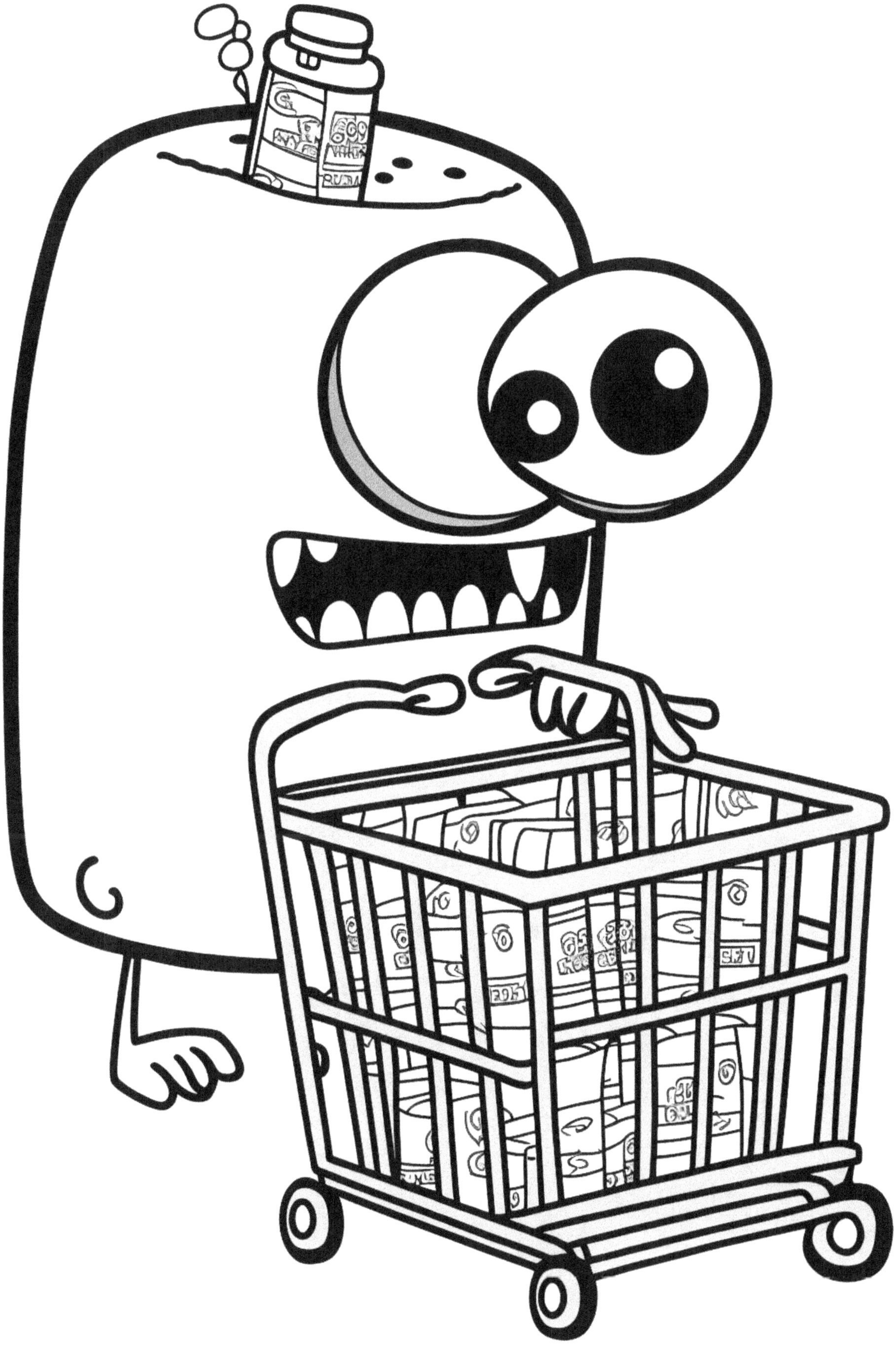

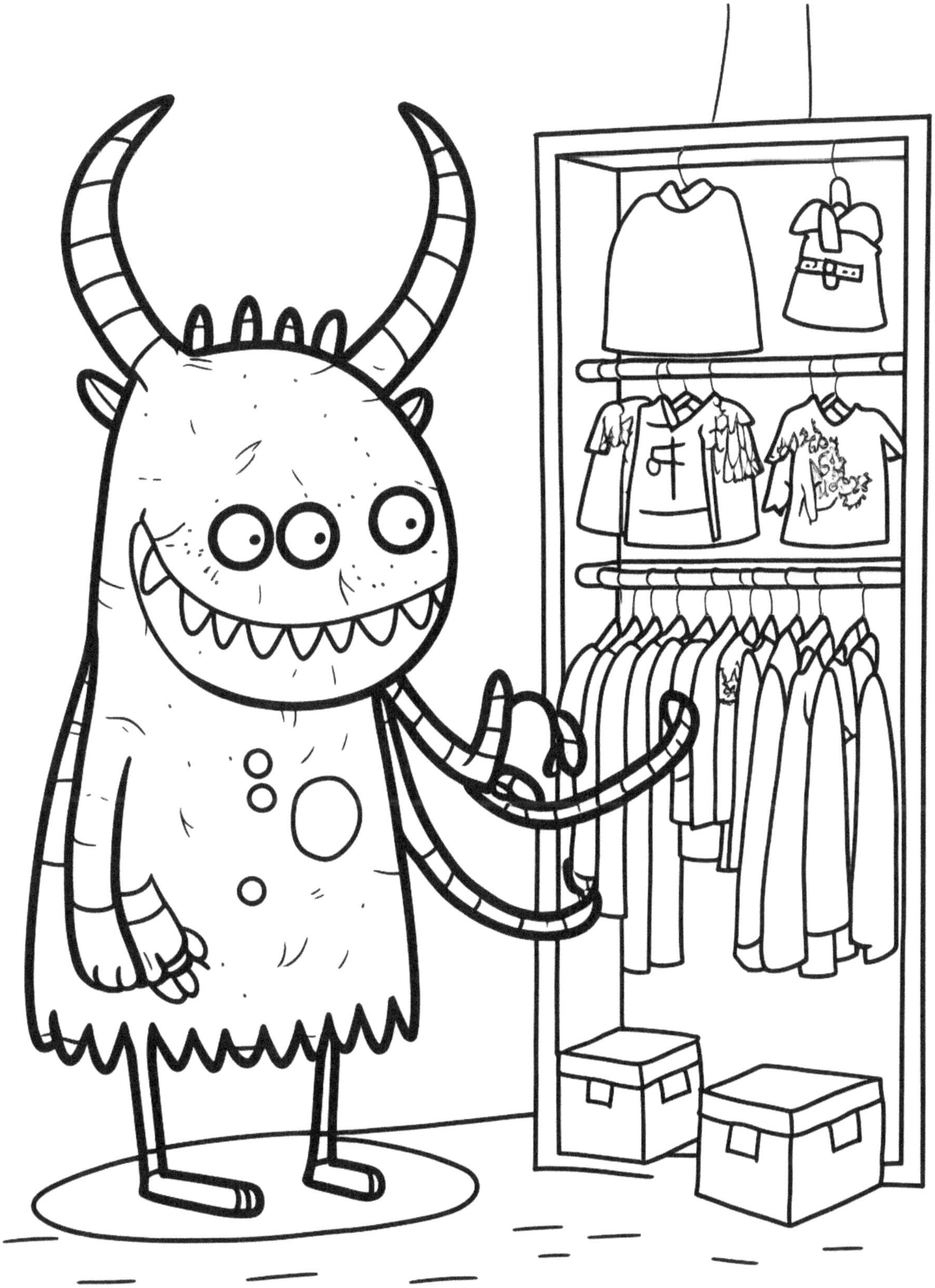

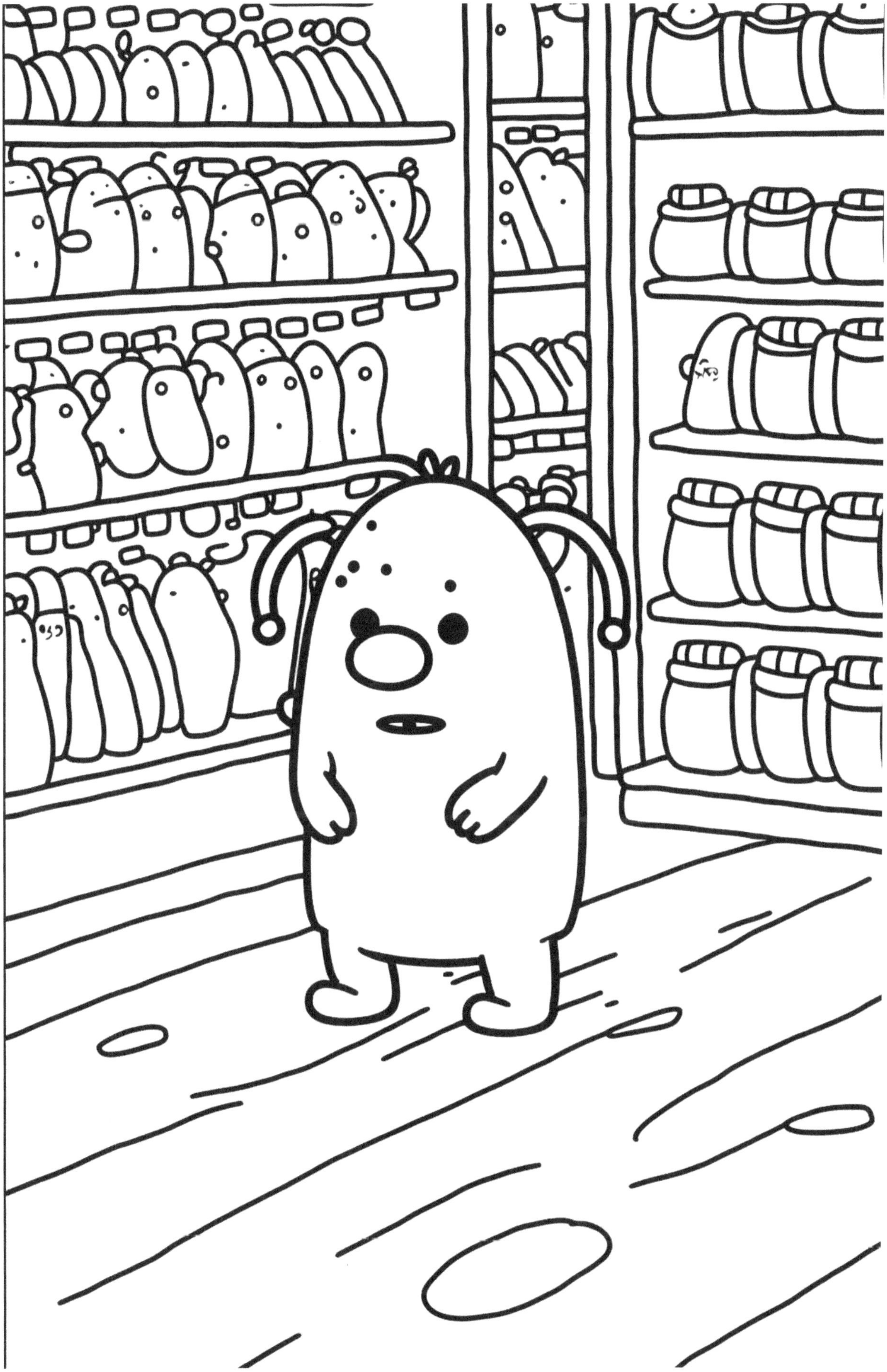

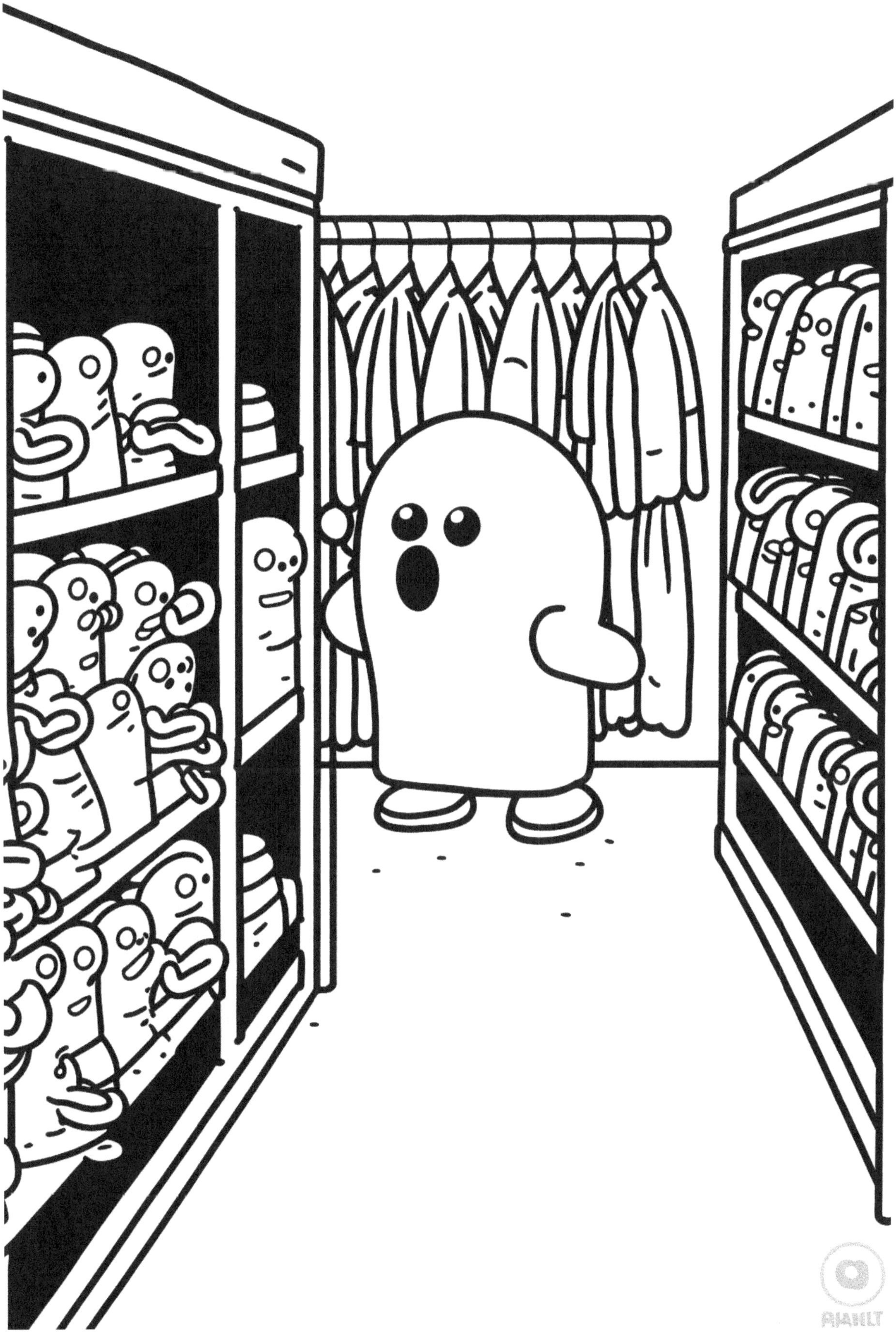

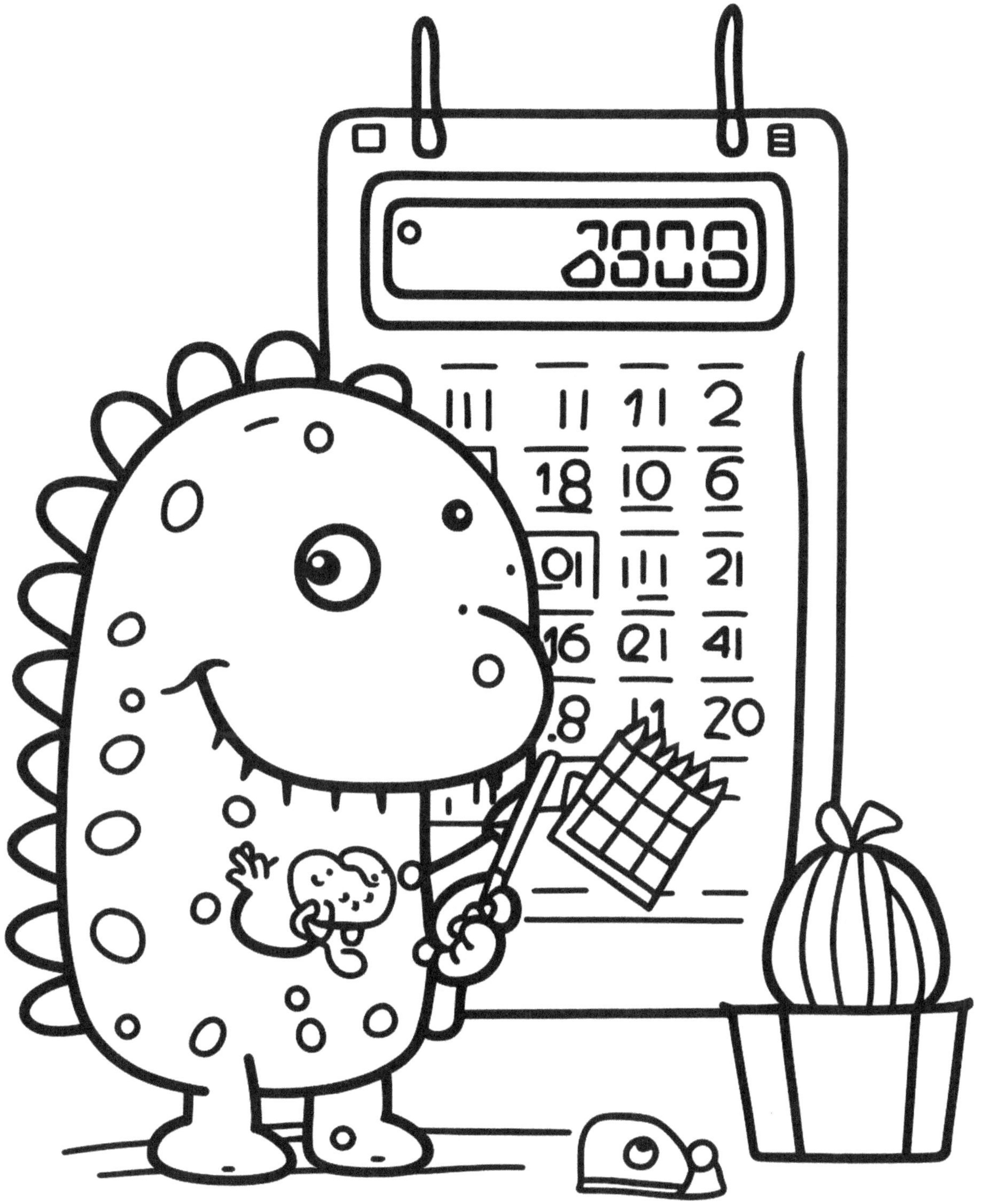

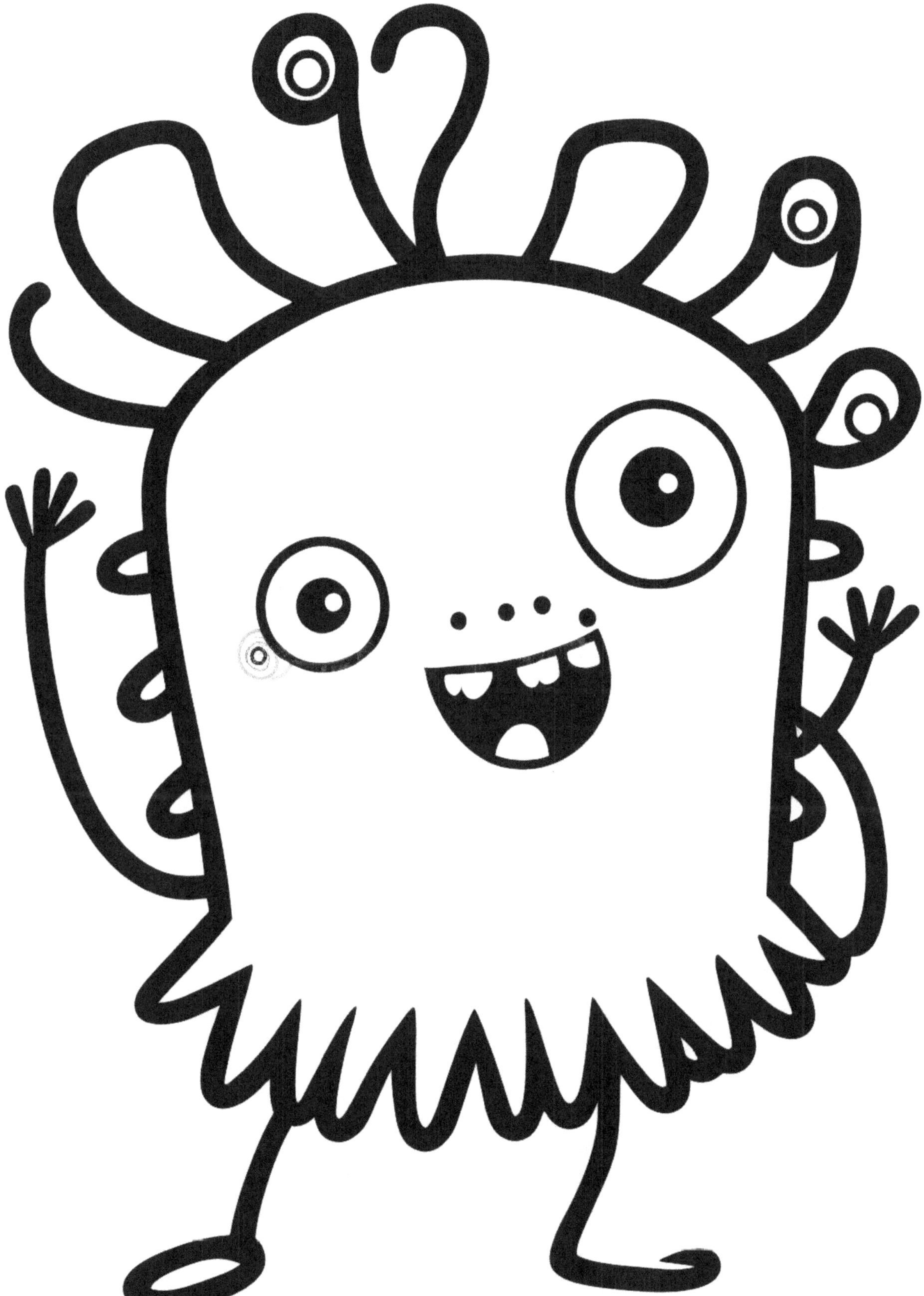

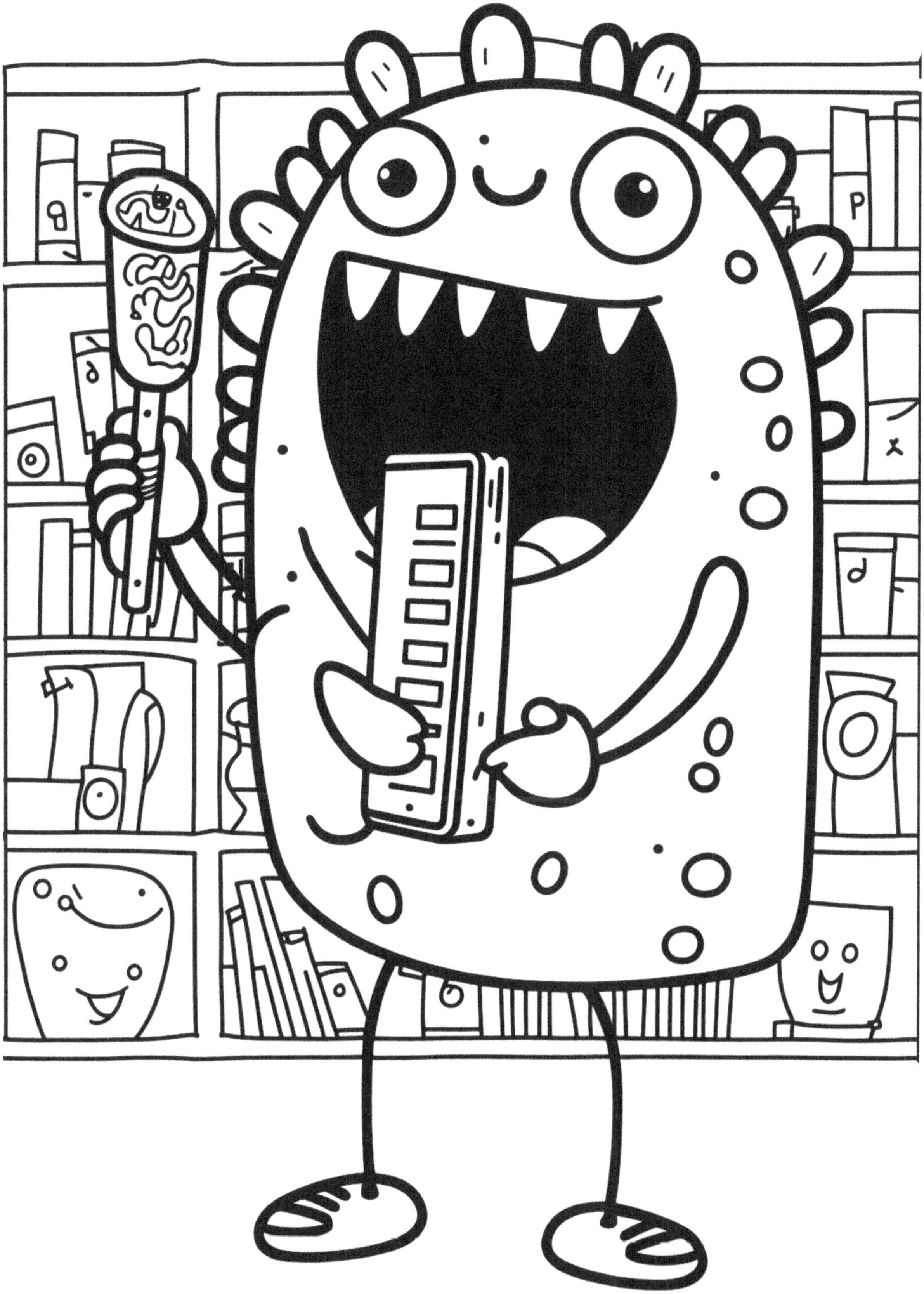

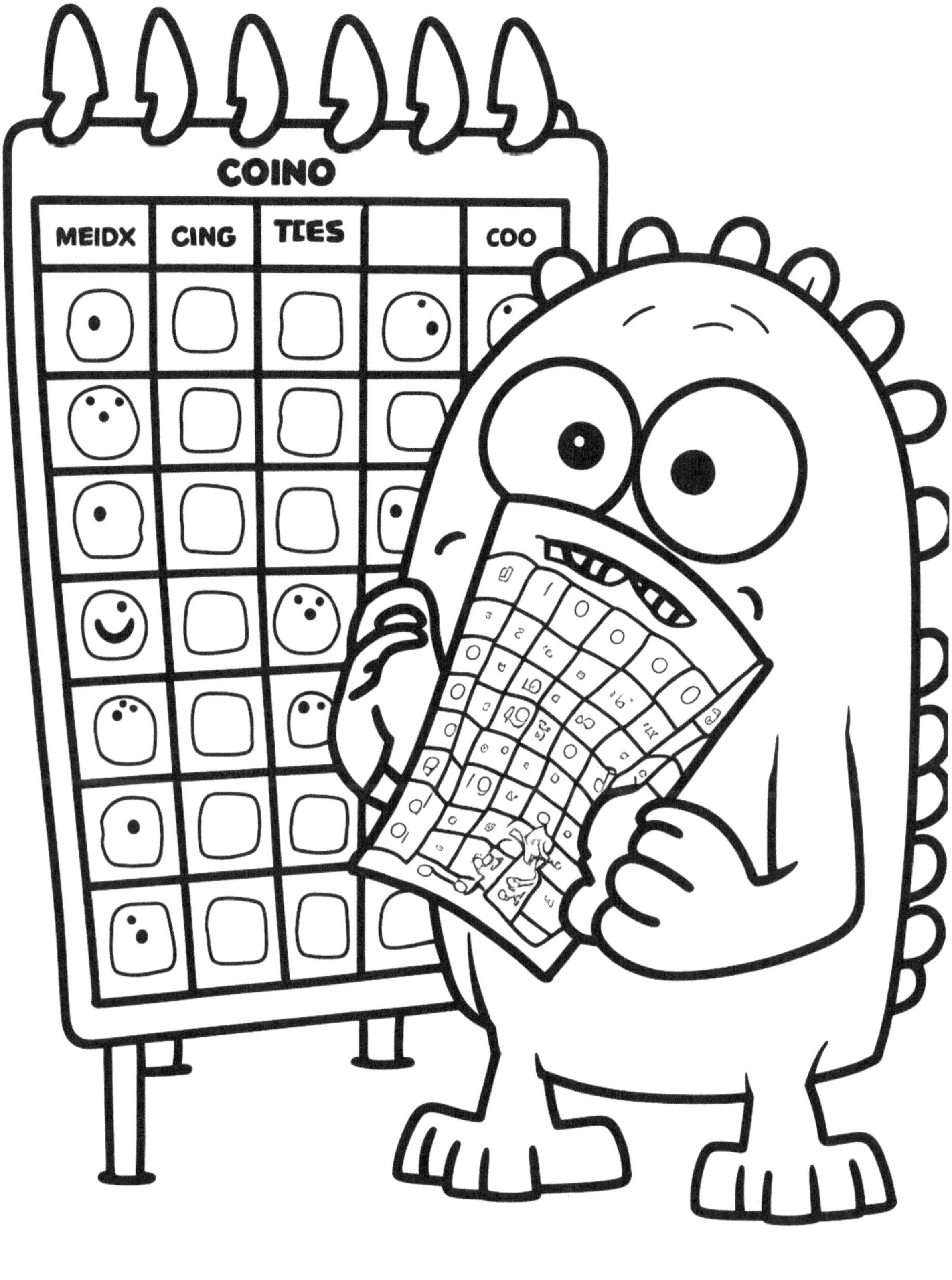

OTTPOLRONUDRN OOCCO

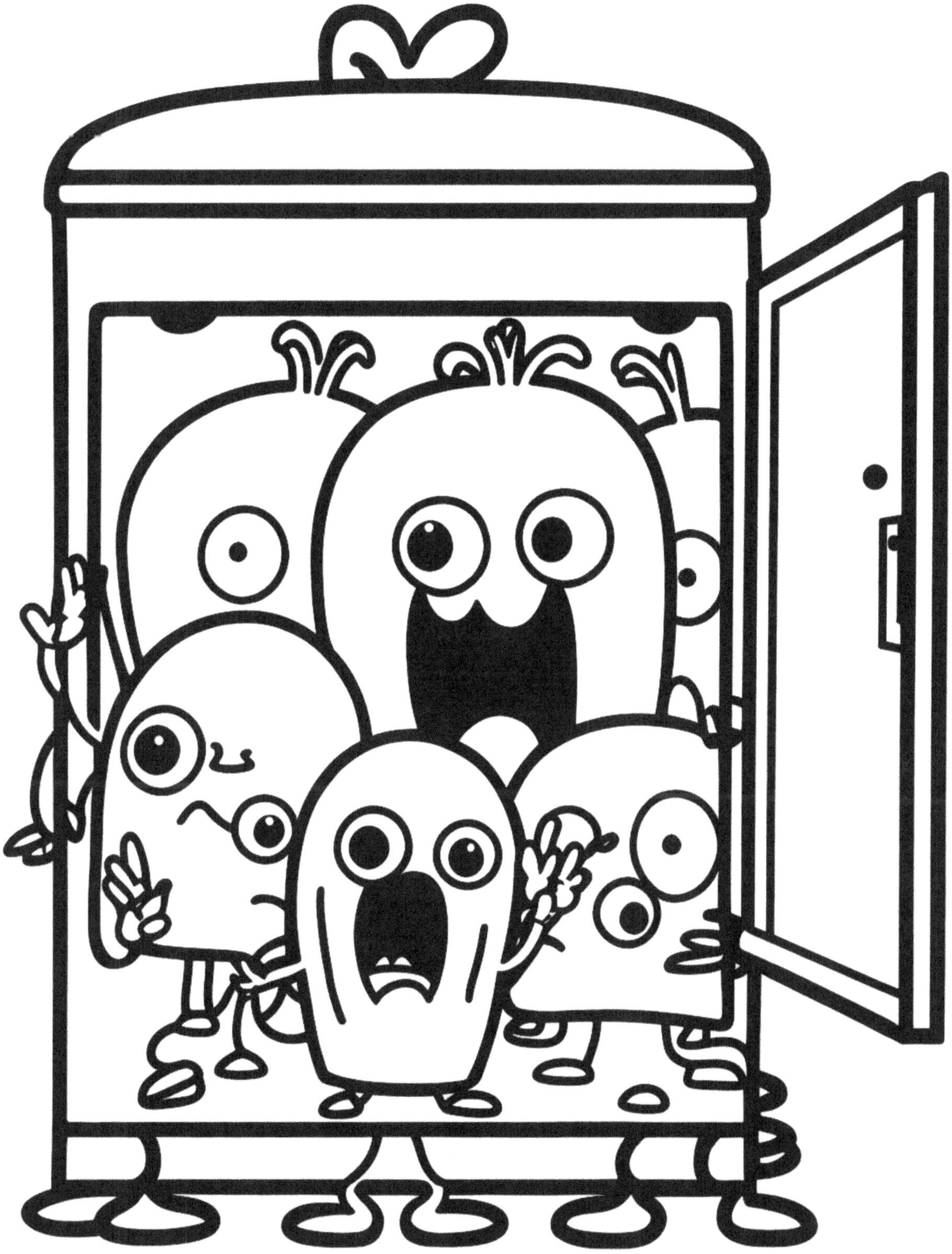

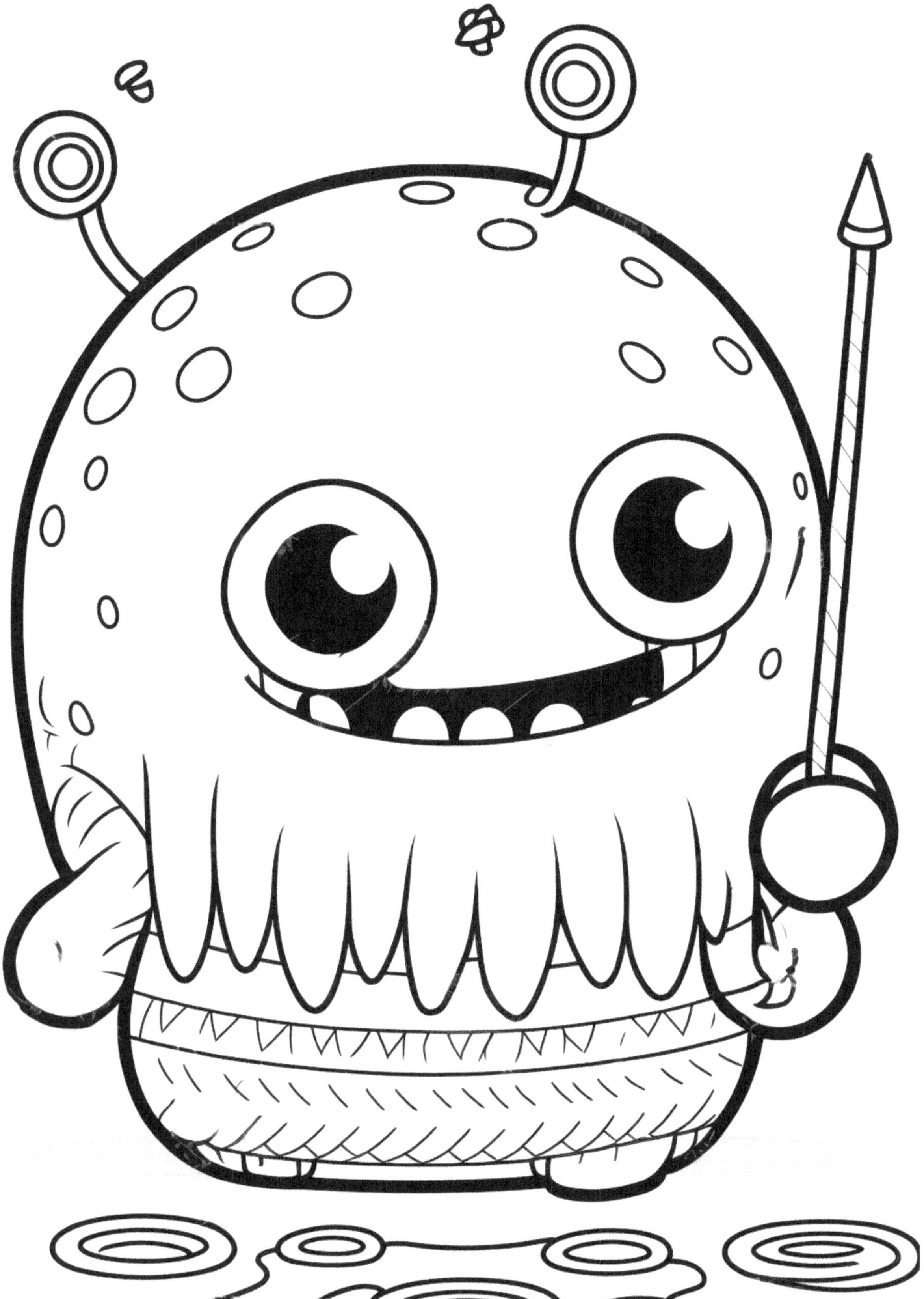

www.ingramcontent.com/pod-product-compliance
Lightning Source LLC
Chambersburg PA
CBHW082228290526
45794CB00009B/3722